CLARINET

The **BIG BOOK** of
clarinet songs

AVAILABLE FOR:
Flute, Clarinet, Alto Sax, Tenor Sax, Trumpet,
Horn, Trombone, Violin, Viola, and Cello

ISBN 978-1-4234-2664-6

Visit Hal Leonard Online at
www.halleonard.com

Contact us:
Hal Leonard
7777 West Bluemound Road
Milwaukee, WI 53213
Email: info@halleonard.com

In Europe, contact:
Hal Leonard Europe Limited
42 Wigmore Street
Marylebone, London, W1U 2RN
Email: info@halleonardeurope.com

In Australia, contact:
Hal Leonard Australia Pty. Ltd.
4 Lentara Court
Cheltenham, Victoria, 3192 Australia
Email: info@halleonard.com.au

CONTENTS

4

ALL MY LOVING
from A HARD DAY'S NIGHT

CLARINET

Words and Music by JOHN LENNON
and PAUL McCARTNEY

ALL THE SMALL THINGS

CLARINET

Words and Music by TOM DE LONGE
and MARK HOPPUS

Bright driving Rock

ALLEY CAT

CLARINET

By FRANK BJORN

Moderately slow

ANOTHER ONE BITES THE DUST

Clarinet

Words and Music by
JOHN DEACON

AMERICA
from the Motion Picture THE JAZZ SINGER

CLARINET

Words and Music by
NEIL DIAMOND

ANY DREAM WILL DO

from JOSEPH AND THE AMAZING TECHNICOLOR® DREAMCOAT

Clarinet

Music by ANDREW LLOYD WEBBER
Lyrics by TIM RICE

BE TRUE TO YOUR SCHOOL

CLARINET

Words and Music by BRIAN WILSON
and MIKE LOVE

Slowly

BAD DAY

CLARINET

Words and Music by
DANIEL POWTER

D.S. al Coda

CODA

BARELY BREATHING

CLARINET

Words and Music by
DUNCAN SHEIK

(It's A)
BEAUTIFUL MORNING

CLARINET

Words and Music by FELIX CAVALIERE
and EDWARD BRIGATI, JR.

BEAUTY AND THE BEAST

from Walt Disney's BEAUTY AND THE BEAST

Clarinet

Lyrics by HOWARD ASHMAN
Music by ALAN MENKEN

Moderately slow

BEYOND THE SEA

CLARINET

Words and Music by CHARLES TRENET,
ALBERT LASRY and JACK LAWRENCE

BLACKBIRD

CLARINET

Words and Music by JOHN LENNON
and PAUL McCARTNEY

BLUE SUEDE SHOES

Clarinet

Words and Music by
CARL LEE PERKINS

BOOGIE WOOGIE BUGLE BOY
from BUCK PRIVATES

CLARINET

Words and Music by DON RAYE
and HUGHIE PRINCE

THE BRADY BUNCH

Theme from the Paramount Television Series THE BRADY BUNCH

Clarinet

Words and Music by SHERWOOD SCHWARTZ
and FRANK DEVOL

BUTTERFLY KISSES

Clarinet

Words and Music by BOB CARLISLE
and RANDY THOMAS

BREAKING FREE
from the Disney Channel Original Movie HIGH SCHOOL MUSICAL

CLARINET

Words and Music by
JAMIE HOUSTON

Moderately

CABARET
from the Musical CABARET

Words by FRED EBB
Music by JOHN KANDER

CLARINET

CALIFORNIA DREAMIN'

Clarinet

Words and Music by JOHN PHILLIPS
and MICHELLE PHILLIPS

CANDLE IN THE WIND

Clarinet

Words and Music by ELTON JOHN
and BERNIE TAUPIN

CHIM CHIM CHER-EE

from Walt Disney's MARY POPPINS

Clarinet

Words and Music by RICHARD M. SHERMAN
and ROBERT B. SHERMAN

CLOCKS

Clarinet

Words and Music by GUY BERRYMAN, JON BUCKLAND,
WILL CHAMPION and CHRIS MARTIN

(They Long to Be)
CLOSE TO YOU

CLARINET

Lyric by HAL DAVID
Music by BURT BACHARACH

COLORS OF THE WIND
from Walt Disney's POCAHONTAS

CLARINET

Music by ALAN MENKEN
Lyrics by STEPHEN SCHWARTZ

COME FLY WITH ME

CLARINET

Words by SAMMY CAHN
Music by JAMES VAN HEUSEN

COPACABANA
(At the Copa)
from Barry Manilow's COPACABANA

CLARINET

Music by BARRY MANILOW
Lyric by BRUCE SUSSMAN and JACK FELDMAN

DO-RE-MI
from THE SOUND OF MUSIC

Clarinet

Lyrics by OSCAR HAMMERSTEIN II
Music by RICHARD RODGERS

DO WAH DIDDY DIDDY

CLARINET

Words and Music by JEFF BARRY
and ELLIE GREENWICH

(Sittin' On)
THE DOCK OF THE BAY

CLARINET

Words and Music by STEVE CROPPER
and OTIS REDDING

DON'T BE CRUEL
(To a Heart That's True)

Clarinet

Words and Music by OTIS BLACKWELL
and ELVIS PRESLEY

DON'T LET THE SUN GO DOWN ON ME

CLARINET

Words and Music by ELTON JOHN
and BERNIE TAUPIN

Slow Rock

DON'T SPEAK

CLARINET

Words and Music by ERIC STEFANI
and GWEN STEFANI

DRIFT AWAY

CLARINET

Words and Music by
MENTOR WILLIAMS

DUKE OF EARL

CLARINET

Words and Music by EARL EDWARDS,
EUGENE DIXON and BERNICE WILLIAMS

THEME FROM E.T. (THE EXTRA-TERRESTRIAL)

from the Universal Picture E.T. (THE EXTRA-TERRESTRIAL)

CLARINET

Music by
JOHN WILLIAMS

EDELWEISS
from THE SOUND OF MUSIC

Clarinet

Lyrics by OSCAR HAMMERSTEIN II
Music by RICHARD RODGERS

EVERY BREATH YOU TAKE

CLARINET

Music and Lyrics by
STING

EVERYTHING IS BEAUTIFUL

CLARINET

Words and Music by
RAY STEVENS

FALLIN'

CLARINET

Words and Music by
ALICIA KEYS

49

FIELDS OF GOLD

CLARINET

Music and Lyrics by
STING

Flowing

FLY LIKE AN EAGLE

CLARINET

Words and Music by
STEVE MILLER

FOR ONCE IN MY LIFE

Clarinet

Words by RONALD MILLER
Music by ORLANDO MURDEN

FOREVER YOUNG

Clarinet

Words and Music by ROD STEWART,
JIM CREGAN, KEVIN SAVIGAR and BOB DYLAN

FUN, FUN, FUN

CLARINET

Words and Music by BRIAN WILSON
and MIKE LOVE

THE GIRL FROM IPANEMA
(Garôta de Ipanema)

Clarinet

Music by ANTONIO CARLOS JOBIM
English Words by NORMAN GIMBEL
Original Words by VINICIUS DE MORAES

Bossa Nova

GOD BLESS THE U.S.A

CLARINET

Words and Music by
LEE GREENWOOD

GONNA BUILD A MOUNTAIN

from the Musical Production STOP THE WORLD – I WANT TO GET OFF

Clarinet

Words and Music by LESLIE BRICUSSE
and ANTHONY NEWLEY

Moderately bright

GOODBYE YELLOW BRICK ROAD

CLARINET

Words and Music by ELTON JOHN
and BERNIE TAUPIN

Moderately slow, in 2

GREEN GREEN GRASS OF HOME

CLARINET

Words and Music by
CURLY PUTMAN

HAPPY DAYS
Theme from the Paramount Television Series HAPPY DAYS

Clarinet

Words by NORMAN GIMBEL
Music by CHARLES FOX

HAVE I TOLD YOU LATELY

CLARINET

Words and Music by
VAN MORRISON

HEART AND SOUL

from the Paramount Short Subject A SONG IS BORN

Clarinet

Words by FRANK LOESSER
Music by HOAGY CARMICHAEL

Moderately, lightly rhythmical

HOGAN'S HEROES MARCH
from the Television Series HOGAN'S HEROES

Clarinet

By JERRY FIELDING

HERE WITHOUT YOU

CLARINET

Words and Music by MATT ROBERTS,
BRAD ARNOLD, CHRISTOPHER HENDERSON
and ROBERT HARRELL

I DREAMED A DREAM

from LES MISÉRABLES

Clarinet

Music by CLAUDE-MICHEL SCHÖNBERG
Lyrics by ALAIN BOUBLIL, JEAN-MARC NATEL
and HERBERT KRETZMER

I HEARD IT THROUGH THE GRAPEVINE

Clarinet

Words and Music by NORMAN J. WHITFIELD
and BARRETT STRONG

I SAY A LITTLE PRAYER

CLARINET

Lyric by HAL DAVID
Music by BURT BACHARACH

Moderately fast

I WHISTLE A HAPPY TUNE

from THE KING AND I

Clarinet

Lyrics by OSCAR HAMMERSTEIN II
Music by RICHARD RODGERS

I WILL REMEMBER YOU
Theme from THE BROTHERS McMULLEN

Clarinet

Words and Music by SARAH McLACHLAN,
SEAMUS EGAN and DAVE MERENDA

I WRITE THE SONGS

Clarinet

Words and Music by
BRUCE JOHNSTON

Slow Ballad

I'M POPEYE THE SAILOR MAN

Theme from the Paramount Cartoon POPEYE THE SAILOR

CLARINET

Words and Music by
SAMMY LERNER

IF I EVER LOSE MY FAITH IN YOU

CLARINET

Music and Lyrics by
STING

IMAGINE

CLARINET

Words and Music by
JOHN LENNON

Medium slow

IT'S MY LIFE

Clarinet

Words and Music by JON BON JOVI,
RICHARD SAMBORA and MARTIN SANDBERG

IT'S STILL ROCK AND ROLL TO ME

CLARINET

Words and Music by
BILLY JOEL

Moderately fast Rock Shuffle

JAILHOUSE ROCK

Clarinet

Words and Music by JERRY LEIBER
and MIKE STOLLER

JOY TO THE WORLD

Clarinet

Words and Music by
HOYT AXTON

Moderate Gospel Rock

JUMP, JIVE AN' WAIL

CLARINET

Words and Music by
LOUIS PRIMA

KANSAS CITY

CLARINET

Words and Music by JERRY LEIBER
and MIKE STOLLER

KOKOMO
from the Motion Picture COCKTAIL

CLARINET

Moderately bright

Words and Music by MIKE LOVE, TERRY MELCHER,
JOHN PHILLIPS and SCOTT McKENZIE

LET 'EM IN

CLARINET

Words and Music by
PAUL and LINDA McCARTNEY

LET'S STAY TOGETHER

CLARINET

Words and Music by AL GREEN,
WILLIE MITCHELL and AL JACKSON, JR.

LIKE A ROCK

CLARINET

Words and Music by
BOB SEGER

LIVIN' LA VIDA LOCA

Clarinet

Words and Music by ROBI ROSA
and DESMOND CHILD

Fast, with a steady beat

LOVE AND MARRIAGE

CLARINET

Words by SAMMY CAHN
Music by JAMES VAN HEUSEN

LOVE STORY

Theme from the Paramount Picture LOVE STORY

CLARINET

Music by FRANCIS LAI

MAGGIE MAY

Clarinet

Words and Music by ROD STEWART
and MARTIN QUITTENTON

MAKING OUR DREAMS COME TRUE

Theme from the Paramount Television Series LAVERNE AND SHIRLEY

CLARINET

Words by NORMAN GIMBEL
Music by CHARLES FOX

MAYBE I'M AMAZED

Clarinet

Words and Music by
PAUL McCARTNEY

Moderately

small notes optional

MICHELLE

CLARINET

Words and Music by JOHN LENNON
and PAUL McCARTNEY

MICKEY MOUSE MARCH

from Walt Disney's THE MICKEY MOUSE CLUB

Clarinet

Words and Music by
JIMMIE DODD

MISSION: IMPOSSIBLE THEME

From the Paramount Television Series MISSION: IMPOSSIBLE

CLARINET

By LALO SCHIFRIN

Moderately, with drive

MISTER SANDMAN

CLARINET

Lyric and Music by
PAT BALLARD

MOON RIVER

from the Paramount Picture BREAKFAST AT TIFFANY'S

Clarinet

Words by JOHNNY MERCER
Music by HENRY MANCINI

Slowly

MY HEART WILL GO ON
(Love Theme from 'Titanic')
from the Paramount and Twentieth Century Fox Motion Picture TITANIC

Clarinet

Music by JAMES HORNER
Lyric by WILL JENNINGS

Moderately

small notes optional

1.

2.

MY WAY

Clarinet

English Words by PAUL ANKA
Original French Words by GILLES THIBAULT
Music by JACQUES REVAUX and CLAUDE FRANCOIS

NA NA HEY HEY KISS HIM GOODBYE

Clarinet

Words and Music by ARTHUR FRASHUER DALE,
PAUL ROGER LEKA and GARY CARLA

ON BROADWAY

CLARINET

Words and Music by BARRY MANN,
CYNTHIA WEIL, MIKE STOLLER and JERRY LEIBER

PEPPERMINT TWIST

CLARINET

Words and Music by JOSEPH DiNICOLA
and HENRY GLOVER

POCKETFUL OF MIRACLES

CLARINET

Words by SAMMY CAHN
Music by JAMES VAN HEUSEN

PUFF THE MAGIC DRAGON

Clarinet

Words and Music by LENNY LIPTON
and PETER YARROW

Moderately

PUT YOUR HAND IN THE HAND

CLARINET

Words and Music by
GENE MacLELLAN

QUIET NIGHTS OF QUIET STARS
(Corcovado)

Clarinet

English Words by GENE LEES
Original Words and Music by ANTONIO CARLOS JOBIM

Moderately slow

ROCK AROUND THE CLOCK

Clarinet

Words and Music by MAX C. FREEDMAN
and JIMMY DeKNIGHT

ROCK WITH YOU

Clarinet

Words and Music by
ROD TEMPERTON

Moderate Rock

SATIN DOLL

CLARINET

By DUKE ELLINGTON

SAVE THE BEST FOR LAST

Clarinet

Words and Music by PHIL GALDSTON,
JON LIND and WENDY WALDMAN

THEME FROM "SCHINDLER'S LIST"

from the Universal Motion Picture SCHINDLER'S LIST

CLARINET

Music by JOHN WILLIAMS

SHE WILL BE LOVED

CLARINET

Words and Music by ADAM LEVINE
and JAMES VALENTINE

SING
from SESAME STREET

CLARINET

Words and Music by
JOE RAPOSO

Moderately

SO LONG, FAREWELL

from THE SOUND OF MUSIC

Clarinet

Lyrics by OSCAR HAMMERSTEIN II
Music by RICHARD RODGERS

Moderately

small notes optional

1., 2.

3.

Slower

SOMEWHERE OUT THERE
from AN AMERICAN TAIL

Clarinet

Music by BARRY MANN and JAMES HORNER
Lyric by CYNTHIA WEIL

SPANISH FLEA

CLARINET

Words and Music by
JULIUS WECHTER

STACY'S MOM

CLARINET

Words and Music by CHRIS COLLINGWOOD
and ADAM SCHLESINGER

SUNRISE, SUNSET
from the Musical FIDDLER ON THE ROOF

CLARINET

Words by SHELDON HARNICK
Music by JERRY BOCK

Moderately slow Waltz tempo

TAKE MY BREATH AWAY
(Love Theme)
from the Paramount Picture TOP GUN

CLARINET

Words and Music by GIORGIO MORODER
and TOM WHITLOCK

THAT'S AMORÉ
(That's Love)
from the Paramount Picture THE CADDY

CLARINET

Words by JACK BROOKS
Music by HARRY WARREN

THIS LAND IS YOUR LAND

Clarinet

Words and Music by
WOODY GUTHRIE

Moderately bright

THOSE WERE THE DAYS

Clarinet

Words and Music by
GENE RASKIN

TIME AFTER TIME

Clarinet

Words and Music by CYNDI LAUPER
and ROB HYMAN

Moderately fast Rock

A THOUSAND MILES

CLARINET

Words and Music by
VANESSA CARLTON

TOMORROW

from the Musical Production ANNIE

CLARINET

Lyric by MARTIN CHARNIN
Music by CHARLES STROUSE

Moderately slow

TOP OF THE WORLD

Clarinet

Words and Music by JOHN BETTIS
and RICHARD CARPENTER

TWIST AND SHOUT

Clarinet

Words and Music by BERT RUSSELL
and PHIL MEDLEY

UNCHAINED MELODY

Clarinet

Lyric by HY ZARET
Music by ALEX NORTH

UNDER THE BOARDWALK

Clarinet

Words and Music by ARTIE RESNICK
and KENNY YOUNG

UNITED WE STAND

Clarinet

Words and Music by ANTHONY TOBY HILLER
and JOHN GOODISON

THE WAY YOU MOVE

Clarinet

Words and Music by ANTWAN PATTON,
PATRICK BROWN and CARLTON MAHONE

WE ARE THE WORLD

CLARINET

Words and Music by LIONEL RICHIE
and MICHAEL JACKSON

WE BELONG TOGETHER

Clarinet

Words and Music by MARIAH CAREY,
JERMAINE DUPRI, MANUEL SEAL, JOHNTA AUSTIN,
DARNELL BRISTOL, KENNETH EDMONDS, SIDNEY JOHNSON,
PATRICK MOTEN, BOBBY WOMACK and SANDRA SULLY

Slow Soul

To Coda

D.S. al Coda

CODA

WHAT THE WORLD NEEDS NOW IS LOVE

CLARINET

Lyric by HAL DAVID
Music by BURT BACHARACH

WITH A LITTLE HELP FROM MY FRIENDS

CLARINET

Words and Music by JOHN LENNON
and PAUL McCARTNEY

WONDERFUL TONIGHT

CLARINET

Words and Music by
ERIC CLAPTON

WOOLY BULLY

CLARINET

Words and Music by
DOMINGO SAMUDIO

Moderately

small notes optional

YELLOW SUBMARINE

Clarinet

Words and Music by JOHN LENNON
and PAUL McCARTNEY

YOU ARE THE SUNSHINE OF MY LIFE

CLARINET

Words and Music by
STEVIE WONDER

Moderately

YOU RAISE ME UP

Clarinet

Words and Music by BRENDAN GRAHAM
and ROLF LOVLAND

YOU'VE GOT A FRIEND

Clarinet

Words and Music by
CAROLE KING

ZIP-A-DEE-DOO-DAH

from Walt Disney's SONG OF THE SOUTH
from Disneyland and Walt Disney World's SPLASH MOUNTAIN

CLARINET

Words by RAY GILBERT
Music by ALLIE WRUBEL